Come to the Table

Books by Meredith Gould

The Catholic Home:
Celebrations and Traditions for
Holidays, Feast Days, and Every Day
(Doubleday)

Deliberate Acts of Kindness:
Service as a Spiritual Practice
(Doubleday)

Staying Sober:
Tips for Working a
Twelve Step Program of Recovery
(Hazelden)

Working at Home:
Making it Work for You
(Storey)

Come to the Table

A Catholic Passover Seder
for
Holy Week

Meredith Gould

Plowshares Publishing
www.PlowsharesPublishing.com

Princeton, New Jersey

Published by
Plowshares Publishing
www.PlowsharesPublishing.com

Book design by
♨♨♨
www.ThreeBears.com

Library of Congress Cataloging-in-Publication Data
Gould, Meredith, 1951–
Come to the Table: A Catholic Passover Seder for Holy Week
Meredith Gould — 1st ed.

Excerpts from the English language translation of the *Catechism of the Catholic Church* for use in the United States of America ©1994, United States Catholic Conference, Inc. — Libreria Editrice Vaticana. Used with permission. Excerpts from the English translation of the *Catechism of the Catholic Church: Modifications from "Editio Typica"* ©1997, United States Catholic Conference, Inc. — Libreria Editrice Vaticana. Used with permission.

ISBN 0-9763962-0-3

Manufactured in the United States of America

January 2005

First Edition

For my mother, Gerry Gould, who
believes in the Believers ... as well as correct syntax.

"Many women do noble things, but you surpass them all."
PROVERBS 31:29

CONTENTS

PREFACE

I WAS already past forty when a series of events literally brought me to my knees and Jesus, the Rabbi from Nazareth, transformed in my heart and mind into Jesus the Christ. Getting baptized was the next right thing to do and in case you're wondering, I certainly did *not* tell my parents.

Passover continued to change during my years of formation as a Christian and the Catholic I would choose to become. The Passover story and the seder celebration itself took on deeper meaning during that time. Four years after my baptism, I went to a seder where questions asked by another guest, a Christian man, were left unanswered by the Conservative Jewish family who had invited him. I remained silent, ostensibly because I didn't want to embarrass my hosts, and then spent Lent feeling awful that I hadn't fully owned my Christianity.

That was also the year I was at an Easter Sunday dinner where my lapsed-Catholic-now-Christian fundamentalist hosts had cobbled together a set of photocopied readings from Exodus, Deuteronomy, Luke, and John — a haggadah of sorts. I became acutely aware of the hunger I saw among Christians to connect more — and more authentically — with Jewish heritage. I wanted to create a seder service that would help Christians do this, so I started this project, *Come to the Table*, never realizing how it would change during the six years I worked on it.

Whatever understanding and appreciation I had for Passover was shaped by the Passover *seder* (order) of my childhood. That annual seder was always a festive, food-filled, family fracas. We'd read only the first fifty pages of the *haggadah* (telling), thirty of which we skipped because they had pictures, music, and Hebrew no one could read. Even so, our seder always seemed interminably long. I found the 1923 *Union Haggadah* my grandparents insisted on using, with its tiny typeface and gloomy illustrations, just plain boring.

I much preferred the haggadah illustrated by Arthur Szyk with its deep cobalt-blue velvet cover embossed with a gold *Kiddush* cup. I still couldn't read the Hebrew, but Szyk's ornate illumination of that ancient language brought it to life. So did the lavishly colored illustrations. They were magical, captivating, and occasionally terrifying. His visual interpretation of the ten plagues was particularly scary. I loved it. Alas, there was only one treasured copy used more for display than for reading at the table. Back then, my mother stashed it well out of wine-spilling range and even now only lets me borrow it on very temporary loan.

Like other families, we added our own strange and possibly demented traditions to the seder — like the sugar-free, yeast-free tomato soup cake my grandmother insisted on calling a dessert. To this day, there's some dispute as to whether it was awful or awesome. I could always count on major annual arguments about whether the hard-boiled egg should be eaten whole after being dipped, or mashed completely in the salt water. Every year, my grandfather's cousin Rose audibly clicked her tongue against her teeth and announced, "Not the way we did it in Romania."

By my teen years, during the 1960s, I started appreciating the sociopolitical symbolism of Passover as a festival of liberation. During college, "Let my people go" seemed like a good, all-purpose politically correct response to racism, anti-Semitism, sexism, and militarism. It was also around this time I started insisting that our seder dinner include at least one vegetarian entrée. Over the years, my seder attendance waned to zilch, although during my Hindu phase I whooped it up at a fairly exuberant one at an ashram that boasted a critical mass of Jews in residence.

Earlier versions of this Catholic Christian seder were quite different from the one you'll be reading here, and that's because of my ongoing religious formation. As I will tell anyone who asks, I'm a Jew by identity, a Christian by faith, and a Catholic in practice. If anything, my Judaism has been enhanced, rather than diminished, by my Christianity. Without a doubt, my Christianity has been enhanced by my Judaism.

Eventually, I came to understand that my Christian faith was best experienced and expressed through Catholic practice. That's a longer conversation, but here I will say that our focus on the Eucharist, our coming together for the Holy Supper of the Lord, at the Table of the Lord, and our commitment to "go in peace to love and serve the Lord and one another" made Catholicism the obvious choice.

And so, after more than a few Lenten journeys and Triduum experiences as a practicing Catholic, this seder ritual changed again in my heart and in my observance. As a convert from Judaism, I couldn't ignore the fact that the Last Supper was the Last Seder, that Gethsemane and Golgotha would come next. After that? Resurrection and salvation, thanks be to God. But, ever the mystic, I wanted to feel the dark immensity of that Last Seder. And I wanted other Catholics to experience a Passover ritual that would help bring the Judaism of Jesus — and our own — to life. I hope I have helped to do that in *Come to the Table*.

Meredith Gould, Ph.D.

Lent 2004

PREFACE P.S.

My MOTHER thinks the Preface to this haggadah is incomplete. She thinks I haven't conveyed to you the richness Passover holds for Jews.

We're both passionate about our positions and perspectives. She's not keen on my desire to feel the dark immensity of that Last Seder. She wants you to know that Passover is a festival that celebrates the joy of liberation. We've been freed from bondage; what's not to celebrate?

But Mom, I've argued, how much celebration can there be when we know darn well what happens next? You know, all that heinous activity *before* the Resurrection: abandonment at Gethsemane, betrayal by disciples, scourging by Romans, the excruciating trudge to Golgotha. (Writing this sentence now, I recall one of our more hilarious theological exchanges that began with her asking, "You *believe* that stuff?")

This celebration for Jews, she has argued, is about more than simply escaping Egypt over 5,000 years ago. She connects with the staggering reality of knowing that for thousands of years, millions of Jews throughout the world have observed this holiday. She loves knowing that the same words will be read, and that the same ceremonial foods will be blessed and eaten in the same order. "I love this connectedness," she wrote in one of our email exchanges. "I don't demean the 'frivolity.' This is the irreverent reverence that comes from familiarity and fitting in one's own skin, if even for just a few hours. And I do believe that all Jews who observe Passover feel the same."

But Mom, I've argued, how joyful could Jesus have been? After all, the gospels do imply that Jesus knew he'd be betrayed.

And don't you know that she came back with something about the disciples? They, she posited, would've been lighthearted, at least at the start of that Last Seder.

Now, Mommy and I have ascended into *Midrash* (investigation), the Jewish scholarly tradition of interpreting biblical text from both an ethical and devotional point of view. More emails fly back and forth through cyberspace.

"It became the Last Supper when, indeed, it was *his* last supper," she explained. "I suggest that maybe this is another reason even well-informed Christians don't know that the Last Supper was a seder. That this solemn Christian observance evolved from a Jewish festival defies comparison."

I didn't have the heart to go into what Christians did with Shavuot, the Jewish harvest festival that we celebrate as Pentecost.

There's more, of course; just as there always is whenever my mother and I — and indeed any Christian and Jew committed to thinking about these things — agree to talk and disagree. But for here and now I'm content to fulfill my daughterly duty: My mother wants you to know that Passover is a boisterous, joy-filled festival. Consider yourself told and enjoy!

Assumption of Mary, 2004

A better knowledge of the Jewish people's faith and religious life as professed and lived even now can help our better understanding of certain aspects of Christian liturgy. ... The relationship between Jewish liturgy and Christian liturgy, but also their differences in content, are particularly evident in the great feasts of the liturgical year, such as Passover. For Jews, it is the Passover of history, tending toward the future; for Christians, it is the Passover fulfilled in the death and Resurrection of Christ, though always in expectation of its definitive consummation.

CATECHISM OF THE CATHOLIC CHURCH 1096

I

COME TO THE TABLE

MUCH has already happened to recall our Jewish heritage by the time we hear this part of the Eucharistic Prayer at the evening Mass on Holy Thursday:[1]

> And so, Father, we bring you these gifts.
> We ask that you make them holy by the power of your Spirit,
> that they may become the body and blood
> of your Son, our Lord Jesus Christ,
> at whose command we celebrate this Eucharist.
>
> On the night he was betrayed,
> he took bread and gave you thanks and praise.
> He broke the bread, gave it to his disciples, and said:

---

1   From the Eucharistic Prayer III in *The Roman Missal* (International Committee on English in the Liturgy, Inc., 1973).

Take this, all of you, and eat it:
this is my body which will be given up for you.

When the supper was ended, he took the cup.
Again he gave you thanks and praise,
gave the cup to his disciples, and said:
Take this, all of you, and drink from it:
this is the cup of my blood,
the blood of the new and everlasting covenant.
It will be shed for you and for all
so that sins may be forgiven.
Do this in memory of me.

With these words, we gather at the Table of the Lord to remember and celebrate the point when, during his last Passover seder, Jesus established the Eucharist as a sacrament. From that time forward, the Holy Supper of the Lord would stand at the center of the Christian Mysteries to celebrate what we believe is God's greatest act of salvation.

For thousands of years, the *seder* (Hebrew for "order") has ushered in the annual celebration of Passover for our Jewish forebears including, of course, Jesus of Nazareth and his disciples. This year, too, the Jewish members of God's family will observe Passover with a seder and we will observe Holy Thursday. These different holy days of different religious communions share a connection through Judaism. By illuminating these connections, *Come to the Table: A Catholic Passover Seder for Holy Week* seeks to enrich our appreciation of this shared heritage.

PASSOVER

Although it's not considered one of the High Holy Days of Judaism, Passover is a holiday of central importance. Every spring on the 14th day of the month of Nisan, Jews remember and celebrate their exodus from ancient Egypt at a special ceremonial meal. This story of liberation from Egyptian bondage and God's faithfulness to the Israelites[2] is set forth in the *haggadah* (telling), a text that serves as a ritual for worship, a teaching discourse, and a way to sustain memory.

The content of the haggadah — the Exodus story — has endured for thousands of years. Judaic scholars believe the current haggadah has remained basically intact for at least 1,500 years. Even so, it's not at all unusual for text to be modified to interpret world events, or to incorporate linguistic innovations such as inclusive language. In 1972, for example, illustrator Mark Podwal put together a haggadah titled, *Let My People Go* (Macmillan, 1972), to tell the Passover story with reference to the oppression of Soviet Jews. More recently, any number of haggadot have emerged to include references to twenty-first century culture. I mention this because *Come to the Table*, using as it does a traditional seder structure to organize our Catholic Christian observance of the Jewish exodus during Holy Week, falls well within the Jewish tradition of text-tweaking to make a point. Indeed, since Holy Thursday already includes an abundance of liturgically significant activities for Latin Rite Catholics, I recommend offering this seder on Wednesday evening before Holy Thursday, or on a Wednesday evening the week before Holy Week.[3]

---

2   "Israelites" is one pre-exilic term (Hebrew is another) for the Jewish people that you'll see throughout this text. It does not refer to citizens of the modern State of Israel.

HOLY THURSDAY

The evening Mass on Holy Thursday ushers in our Paschal Triduum, the three-day period of devotions that herald Resurrection Sunday (Easter). Holy Thursday is of central importance to Catholic Christians because it commemorates the institution of two sacraments — the Holy Eucharist and Holy Orders — by Jesus during the Last Supper.

In most dioceses, the Chrism Mass takes place earlier in the day. This Mass includes two significant activities. First, the bishop publicly consecrates the oils for the Holy Chrism, the Anointing of the Sick, and for the Catechumenate. Next, the diocese's priests publicly reaffirm their commitment as priests. Links between the Jewish Passover celebration and our commemoration of the Last Supper become most evident at the evening Mass.

At that Mass, a reading from the Book of Exodus recapitulates God's instructions to Moses and Aaron about escaping from Egypt. We sing Psalm 116:12–19, one of the *hallel* (praise) psalms traditionally recited during the seder, adding this antiphon: "Our blessing-cup is a communion with the Blood of Christ."

After the Gospel reading and before we come to the Lord's table, the presiding priest washes the feet of twelve parishioners to commemorate Jesus' profound act of humility (John 13:1–15). This action has its parallel in the seder's *rachatz* (Blessing the Washing of Hands). After the Liturgy of the Holy Eucharist, the Blessed Sacrament is carried out and reserved in another sacred place so that the church will be starkly empty for the liturgies of the Lord's suffering, death, burial, and awaiting resurrection.

---

3   The Sabbath and, indeed, all Jewish days begin at sundown. We see this Jewish legacy sustained in Vigil Masses that precede our significant holy days (e.g., Christmas Eve Vigil, Easter Vigil).

HISTORICAL TENSIONS

Since the first century, Christians and Jews have shared a difficult and painful history of faith and human reactions to that faith. Here, I cannot provide a comprehensive history of social, political, and theological tensions during the first century. But I will point out that even the least scripturally educated Christian knows that the convert Pharisee Paul, frustrated by repeated rejection by fellow Jews of his preaching Jesus as Messiah, found a more welcoming audience among some gentiles.[4] The great turning point for the development of Christianity occurred when Paul preached that these gentiles would be welcomed into fellowship through baptism alone, rather than through circumcision *and* baptism. Before then, there were simply — or not so simply — Jews of different sects, including Jewish Christians.[5]

---

4   For the story in scripture of Paul's key role in evangelizing the gentiles, read: Acts of the Apostles; for his attitudes and beliefs about the role and value of Jewish law, especially regarding Gentile Christians read: Romans, 1 Thessalonians, Galatians, 2 Corinthians, and Philippians. For scripture about attempts to reinforce the nascent faith of Jewish Christians who were enduring persecution, read: Hebrews. You can find an extensive theological discussion about the pastoral challenges Paul faced with both Jewish and Gentile Christians in Daniel J. Harrington, S.J., *Paul on the Mystery of Israel* (The Liturgical Press, 1992).

5   By the time Jesus of Nazareth was born, Judaism was dominated by two sects, known as the *Sadducees* and *Pharisees*. Their different perspectives about the validity of oral v. written text, viz., Torah, (The Five Books of Moses) is interesting to note.

    The Sadducees vehemently rejected anything that was not part of the written code of the Pentateuch and were extremely tied to temple worship and ritual. The Pharisees, however, viewed Jewish law as a code that should be changed, through extensive oral debate and commentary, to accommodate changing social conditions. They were the predecessors of the scholars that developed the Talmud, a compilation of Torah inquiries and teachings completed by the end of the 6th century CE. The Pharisees also believed in life after death and the world to come, while the Sadducees rejected that teaching as well.

In many ways, Passover and, by extension, Holy Thursday, provides a focus for understanding many subsequent interfaith tensions, not to mention outright violence against Jews, especially during Lent and Easter. The source of anti-Judaism among Christians can be traced to language found in the Eucharistic prayer recalled at the beginning of this chapter, *viz.*, Jesus' declaration: "...this is the cup of my blood, the blood of the new and everlasting covenant," and language within the Passover seder, "The blood will be a sign for you on the houses where you are; and when I see the blood, I will pass over you" (Exodus 12:13).

These words in particular would inspire centuries of "blood libels," accusations especially rampant during the Middle Ages, that Jews slaughter Christian boys during Passover, and then use their

---

Jesus as Rabbi, with his radical teachings about the need for flexibility and accommodation in Jewish law (*halakhah*), was most likely aligned with the Pharisees. His challenges to the law would have been well within the tradition of debate and argument, making the historical fixation on the Pharisees as responsible for killing Christ quite strange. See also: CCC 577-582 (Jesus and the Law); 583-586 (Jesus and the Temple); and 595-597 (The Trial of Jesus).

6   For a chronicle of anti-Judaism during 2,000 years of Church history, read James Carroll, *Constantine's Sword: The Church and the Jews* (Houghton Mifflin, 2001). Carroll, a former Catholic priest, is also a novelist, so the text is sweeping and compelling, although not necessarily accepted by all scholars as valid.

7   Religious historians offer a persuasive political economic theory for the origins and persistence of blood libels, referencing the fact that it was to Christians' religious, political, and economic advantage to have Jewish bankers handle the messy business of lending money and charging interest. This was especially convenient for Christian European rulers who needed to fund wars.

"But when the money was borrowed, at interest, and then the war was lost, what was a good Catholic ruler to do, when he had no wherewithal to pay? Stir up a blood libel accusation somewhere, followed by a few riots and pogroms, and then settle the body politic by declaring the Jews forfeit their assets, and/or the kings absolved of their debts. All of this led the Christians to have very cogent, tangible roots for their latent (and rampant) anti-Semitic resentments. People who are not really very religious are not motivated by hostilities that are very religious. Instead, they use these hostilities as covers for hostilities that are simply venal. We

blood to bake *matzoh* (unleavened bread). Overwrought Passion plays, historically staged during Lent, also provided inspiration (and rationale) for slaughtering Jews as late as the twentieth century.[6,7] Fears about anti-Jewish reprisals were triggered as recently as 2004 with the release of Mel Gibson's movie, *The Passion of the Christ* that, as it turned out, did not stimulate a surge of anti-Judaism in the United States.

The anti-Judaism of the Spanish Inquisition during the 17th century, and the pogroms of Eastern Europe during the 19th century were eclipsed by the virulent anti-Semitism[8] of Hitler's Nazis who sought to exterminate the entire Jewish population of Europe during the 1940s.[9]

Seemingly more benign, but no less pernicious has been ongo-

should also appreciate what a deep yet unexpressed resentment this would impose on the souls of the Jewish communities, who had nowhere to go and no way to express their outrage."
(Personal correspondence to author from Fr. James T. Burtchaell, C.S.C., August 2, 2003.)

8   The Nazi emphasis on Jews as an inferior race that should be exterminated is what characterizes their actions as "anti-Semitic." Earlier attempts to eradicate the Jewish people were tied more to Christian antipathy toward the religion and most specifically Judaism's rejection of Jesus as Christ, hence the term "anti-Judaism" to describe these acts of persecution.

9   Public debate about Catholic complicity at the highest levels of the Church was especially triggered by the proposed beatification of Pope Pius XII in 1965. More than 30 years later, this debate flared up again with publication of *Hitler's Pope: The Secret History of Pius XII* (Viking, 1999). Author John Cornwell acquired access to Vatican documents that he initially believed would exonerate Pius XII from charges of Nazi complicity, only to discover that he would need to write quite a different book.

Cornwell's view of history has been vigorously challenged by Catholic and Jewish historians. For a detailed examination of the Vatican archives, see: *Pius XII and the Second World War: According to the Archives of the Vatican* (Paulist Press, 1999), edited by Peter Blet et al.; Michael O'Carroll, *Pius XII, Greatness Dishonored* (Franciscan Press, 1981). For a layperson's overview of the debate, visit Christopher McGath's page, "Pius XII and the Holocaust" at http://members.aol.com/cmcginmd/PiusXII_Holocaust.htm.

ing theological dickering over the number and nature of covenants made by God. Did this "new and everlasting covenant" transfer God's favor from the Jewish people to Christians? Did God make only one covenant that was finally fulfilled by Jesus Christ? Can and do earlier and later covenants coexist?[10] This debate persists among some theologians, although the most recent Vatican edition of the *Catechism of the Catholic Church* (CCC) states without equivocation that "the Old Covenant has never been revoked" (CCC 121).

RECONCILIATION AND *TESHUVA*

Reading the current official catechism, you'd never suspect this sorrowful history of interfaith enmity. The Church's longstanding biblical and theological debt to Judaism is referenced throughout the huge volume. The Israelites are recognized as "elder brethren" (CCC 63) and the Hebrew Scriptures reaffirmed as "an indispensable part of Sacred Scripture..." (CCC 121). Jesus and his public ministry are properly situated within the historical context that gave rise to "the religious authorities in Jerusalem, whom the Gospel according to John, often calls simply 'the Jews'" (CCC 574), and the Catechism boldly states that "Jews are not collectively responsible for Jesus' death" (CCC 597). The catechism also includes text promulgated as a result of the Second Vatican Council (1962-1965), from the document commonly known as the *Nostra aetate* (CCC 597).

The pope responsible for this radical change in attitude, thought, and behavior toward the Jewish people and Judaism was, of course, Pope John XXIII whose call for *aggoriornamento* (updating)

---

10   For a thorough, albeit head spinning, survey of 20th century theological (Catholic and Protestant) debates about Jesus, the "Christ Event," and Judaism, take a look at: John Pawlikowski, O.S.M., *Jesus and the Theology of Israel* (Michael Glazier, Inc.,1989). His footnotes will lead you to primary sources for discussions that only a seminary student or biblical scholar would have the wherewithal to plumb.

throughout the Church brought revolutionary changes. Thus, it came to pass that in section 4 of "The Declaration of the Relationship of the Church to Non-Christian Religions," a centuries-long history was overturned.

The Nostra aetate repudiates a number of persistent lies. First, it acknowledges the Church's origins in "the patriarchs, Moses, and the prophets." Next, it repudiated displacement or replacement theology by noting the "grafted" on nature of gentile participation in the early Church: "The Church believes that Christ who is our peace has through his cross reconciled Jews and gentiles and made them one in himself." The text underscores the Judaism of the early disciples of Jesus and apostles who first proclaimed the Gospel. It encourages interfaith discussion and declares that regarding the trial and crucifixion of Jesus, "neither all Jews indiscriminately at the time, nor Jews today, can be charged with the crimes committed during this Passion."

But these statements, long overdue, would not immediately change long-held prejudices. In fact, I'm old enough not only to remember when this statement was issued, but also the general response of Jews at the time, which was more along the lines of "we told you so," rather than gratitude for something we always believed. Still to come were actions to reinforce these declarations.

In 1967, the Bishops' Committee for Ecumenical and Interreligious Affairs (BCEIA) issued guidelines for Catholic–Jewish Relations. These guidelines, revised and approved by the BCEIA on April 9, 1985, and authorized for publication by Msgr. Daniel F. Hoye, General Secretary, NCCB/USCC, sought to encourage interfaith dialogue, enhance sensitivity to the Jewish historical experience, eliminate proselytism, and develop catechetical materials to emphasize our shared heritage.

The work of reconciliation begun by Pope John XXIII was continued by Pope John Paul II who, on April 13, 1986, became the first pope in 2,000 years to enter the synagogue of Rome. During his reign, Pope John Paul II performed even more acts of *teshuva* (repentance). He established diplomatic relations between the Vatican City state and the political state of Israel in 1993. In that same year, he responded to accusations that the Church was trying to christianize the Holocaust (*Shoah*). He relocated a group of Carmelite nuns who had set up a convent of prayer at Auschwitz, the former Nazi death camp where Edith Stein, Jewish convert, Carmelite nun, and later canonized St. Teresa Benedicta of the Cross, was gassed to death in 1942.

In 1998, the Pontifical Commission for Religious Relations with the Jews issued "We Remember: A Reflection on the Shoah." A remarkable *mea culpa* document,[11] We Remember confessed the Church's sins of passivity and asked for forgiveness. And continuing into this, the twenty-first century, Pope John Paul II not only visited the Holy Land, but also prayed at the Western (formerly, "Wailing") Wall, the last vestige of the grand Second Temple of Jerusalem that was destroyed by the Romans in 70 CE.

Are these very public admissions and acts of reconciliation enough to heal ancient injuries and rifts? The Jewish precept of teshuva, with its emphasis on apologizing and begging forgiveness, suggests that they might be. But this notion of returning to God after sinning requires more than verbal apology. It also requires intentional action.

The revered twelfth-century Jewish philosopher, Moses Maimonides (Moshe ben Maimon), argued that the sincerity of a penitent offender, in addition to being manifest in refusing to repeat an

---

11   For one review of the theological issues raised by the Pope's mea culpa, take a look at Avery Dulles, "Should the Church Repent?" First Things (December 1998):36-41.

offense given the opportunity, would be enhanced even more by offering compensation for past injuries. True teshuva, then, requires a desire and determination to break completely with past attitudes and behaviors.

In its 1998 document, after reviewing its complicity in crimes against the Jewish people, the Vatican declared, "The Catholic Church therefore repudiates every persecution against a people or human group anywhere, at any time. She absolutely condemns all forms of genocide, as well as the racist ideologies that give rise to them...the spoiled seeds of anti-Judaism and anti-Semitism must never again be allowed to take root in any human heart." This is teshuva and time will tell whether our Church and her people will make good on this pope's mandate.

Meanwhile, I suggest we pay closer attention to what Catholics already share with Jewish people regarding ritual and meaning. *Come to the Table* does this by offering a Passover seder that draws inspiration and structure from, but does not replicate, the Jewish seder. Our belief in Jesus as Christ makes simply using the traditional Jewish seder not only inappropriate, but also impossible — we are Christians. So here, you'll be invited to draw upon core Christian precepts to deepen your appreciation of Passover as the historic antecedent of our Holy Week.[12]

To illuminate these connections, I've included excerpts from Christian scripture to the liturgy. Some rituals have been eliminated

---

12   From the *Catechism of the Catholic Church* (CCC 1096): "A better knowledge of the Jewish people's faith and religious life as professed and lived even now can help our better understanding of certain aspects of Christian liturgy. ... The relationship between Jewish liturgy and Christian liturgy, but also their differences in content, are particularly evident in the great feasts of the liturgical year, such as Passover. For Jews, it is the Passover of history, tending toward the future; for Christians, it is the Passover fulfilled in the death and Resurrection of Christ, though always in expectation of its definitive consummation."

altogether (e.g., the search for afikomen; the Dayenu) because our belief in Jesus as Christ stands in opposition to what some of these ritual elements represent. So, for example, the last cup of wine to be blessed and consumed is not — and cannot — be the traditional Cup of Acceptance, but must be Our Cup of Salvation.

Prayers are offered in their weekday (v. *shabbat*) translations. They're also presented in English instead of transliterated Hebrew. Most contemporary haggadot for Reform and Reconstructionist Jews include Hebrew transliterations so participants can at least produce the sound of Hebrew. I've jettisoned this convention for two major reasons. First, is the matter of WWJS — what would Jesus speak? Did he recite ritual prayers in Hebrew at his last seder? Aramaic? In either event, the Catholic laity (and many of its priests) understands neither. My second reason has to do with the confusing and cumbersome nature of Hebrew transliteration. Many Jews can't grasp it and resort to mumbling. Since the point here is to create a fuller understanding of Holy Thursday and a deeper appreciation for our Jewish roots, I've exercised my God-given free will and opted out of transliteration.

USING THIS CATHOLIC PASSOVER SEDER

Church communities as well as individual families can use *Come to the Table*. You'll find basic information in Chapter 2, "Preparing for Passover," as well as specific directions for creating a Passover experience in the appendixes.

Chapter 4, "A Catholic Passover Seder," is the seder. Traditional haggadot are filled with exegeses for contemplation and discussion alongside the main text; I provide this commentary in footnotes. For a more catechetical experience, the leader might want to address all or some of these notes directly. Another option might be to make this haggadah available to participants in advance and encourage them to come to the table with comments and questions. Accompanying passages from Christian scripture may also be read aloud and discussed as time permits. If they aren't, I hope that at some point during Holy Thursday they'll be studied in the great prayer tradition of *lectio divina* in which contemplated text is deeply absorbed by mind and spirit.

As for the time commitment involved, even without dwelling on additional commentary, plan on devoting at least an hour for the first half of the seder. The festive meal, which comes next, may take up to an hour to serve and enjoy. The second half of the seder (and dessert) will take another half hour or so. Yes, this requires a time commitment! I'll certainly never forget the Orthodox seder I attended during the 1970s where, thanks to an abundance of commentary by the presiding rabbi and his students in attendance, the festive meal wasn't served until 1:00 AM!

You'll need to designate someone to lead. In a parish setting, choose someone who garners respect both for reading and crowd control. In this setting especially, consider assigning and distributing readings well in advance. You'll want to give readers ample time to study and contemplate how to read their texts. In the home you may follow the contemporary custom of rotating readers around the holiday table.

If you're the leader, please invite everyone to come to this table with questions. Everyone's seder experience will be enriched by pondering out loud — at least to whomever is seated in proximity.

Psalms are recited as responsorial readings at seders (except when they're chanted in Hebrew). You do, however, have the option of asking someone in music ministry to lead everyone in song using selections from the psalter; try either or both for this seder.

Some Jewish families observe the venerable tradition of skipping rituals and readings for any number of reasons — fidgeting children, aging relatives, and hungry participants come to mind. If time is a factor, go ahead and omit reading: Hallel (Psalms 113 and 114) before the meal, and then the Hallel (Psalms 116 and 118) after the meal.

Finally, there's the matter of fun. I urge you to wrangle an invitation to an authentically Jewish seder to experience how a feast that observes slavery and liberation, death and deliverance can be fun. The irreverence, arcane arguments, and sheer silliness that frequently emerge during seders generally shocks Christian guests, even those who do not immediately connect this ritual meal with the events of Holy Thursday. Our challenge, as Catholics, is how to manage the cognitive dissonance of combining joy with solemnity, something we're challenged to do throughout Lent because we know that on Resurrection Sunday, we celebrate Christ triumphant.

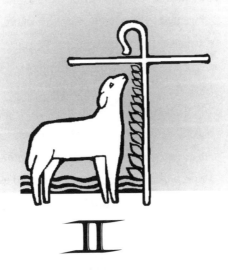

II

Preparing for Passover

THE DAYS before Passover are ones of great preparation. For thousands of years — during inquisitions, pogroms, and massacres, and in secret caves, attic hideouts, and death camps of the Shoah[13] — Jews have gathered during the month of Nisan to celebrate God's promise of freedom from Egyptian bondage.

The rules for Passover preparation are ancient, set forth in Exodus (12:1-20); reiterated in Numbers (9:11-12) and Deuteronomy (16:1-8). Although it may not seem feasible to follow these rules exactly, many are easily observed in modern homes. When we adopt traditional preparations, we join countless others — living, dead, and The One crucified, the Risen — who have celebrated God's faithfulness throughout the ages.

> On the first day of the Feast of Unleavened Bread,
> when it was customary to sacrifice the Passover lamb,
> Jesus' disciples asked him, "Where do you want us to go and
> make preparations for you to eat the Passover?"
> So he sent two of his disciples, telling them,
> "Go into the city and a man carrying a jar of water
> will meet you. Follow him. Say to the owner of the house
> he enters, 'The Rabbi asks: Where is my guest room,
> where I may eat the passover with my disciples?'
> He will show you a large upper room, furnished and ready.
> Make preparations for us there."
> MARK 14:12-15

PREPARING THE HOME
Removing Leaven

In observant Jewish homes, all *hametz* (food made with yeast) is eaten or given away before the holiday begins. Everyday cookware, utensils, dishes, glasses, and flatware are either put away or koshered

---

13   Shoah, also Sho'ah or Shoa (Hebrew for "destruction"), is slowly replacing "Holocaust" to describe Nazi annihilation of Germany's Jewish population during the 1930s, a policy the Nazis pursued in Europe until their defeat in World War II. The original word for holocaust, the Greek *holokauston*, refers to "a burnt sacrifice offered to God" and generally appears in Scripture whenever Torah-mandated sacrifices are mentioned. Christian as well as Jewish theologians are increasingly using Shoah to militate against the theologically offensive implication that the Nazi "Final Solution" had anything to do with pleasing God.

specifically for Passover. Orthodox Jews also store all canned and bottled foods (e.g., spices) to ensure that no hametz survives.

Before the first night of Passover, everybody in the household participates in one final, thorough ceremonial search for hametz. With blessings and a candle lighting their way, the family explores cupboards and closets. Bread and cake crumbs are scooped up with a wooden spoon or brushed into a bag with a feather. In the morning, the head of the family burns the last traces of hametz. Matzoh is the only form of bread or baked goods that may be eaten during Passover.

As Catholics, we pay special attention to food during Lent, which always precedes Passover. Before the Second Vatican Council, devout Catholics renounced eggs, butter, milk, cheese, and meat during the forty days of Lent. Although relatively few contemporary Catholics follow these dietary strictures, we are still asked to set aside certain foods during Lent. Like Jews refraining from eating hametz during Passover, the spiritual discipline of refraining from eating meat during Lent helps us connect abstinence to remembrance. Consider the promise, possibility, and power of also observing this ancient dietary regulation during the Triduum.[14]

---

14 Scholars note that the standards of cleanliness established by the laws of *kashrut* are what spared the Jewish people from a variety of diseases and plagues throughout the centuries.

On the other hand, despite the educated and humane structure of ancient Hebrew society, its hierarchy also used these highly ritualized observances to separate, elevate, or exclude. During his lifetime on earth, the Pharisees and teachers of law challenged Jesus on the laxity with which some of his disciples observed ceremonial washing traditions. In response, Jesus said, "Listen to me, everyone, and understand this. Nothing outside a man can make him unclean by going into him. Rather, it is what comes out of a man that makes him unclean" (Mark 7:1-20).

This debate about which aspects of Torah should or should not be observed to please God continues in Acts of the Apostles (Acts 11:1-18) and is transformed by Paul's successful argument that the Law of Love for all others

PREPARING THE PASSOVER TABLE

Passover is a celebration that delights the senses through prayer, story, song, and food. In Exodus, God invites the Israelites to feast and relax before fleeing Egypt. We're invited to do the same on this holiday, so bring out your best china and family silver. The white tablecloth that's customarily used in Jewish households will be just the right liturgical color for Holy Thursday! God's promise of deliverance and redemption is visible in the season's first flowers, so make room for a lovely bouquet amid platters and candlesticks, even though we won't be seeing flowers in church until Easter Vigil.

Before completing their seder, Jewish celebrants traditionally consume four cups of wine (usually small) to signify the four promises God made to Israel (Exodus 6:6-7). We, too, will include blessing and drinking the "fruit of the vine," so include a wine glass at each place setting. The wine itself should be a sweet red, although the practice of using white wine did emerge during the eighteenth century in an effort to counter blood libels. (Serve grape juice for children and for adults with health issues.)

Have small cushions (or soft pillows) available to everyone. Because Passover celebrates freedom from bondage, participants are encouraged to relax. By custom, participants recline to the left while drinking each cup of wine and eating ceremonial greens, leaving the right hand free to perform these rituals.[15]

---

nullifies any specific proscriptions in Torah. Unclean would become a moral metaphor rather than a ritual technicality or ethnic slur.

Indeed, because of historical and contemporary, as well as theological and practical issues having to do with cleanliness, it makes sense for Christians to omit the second ritual action of the seder, urchatz (washing hands without a blessing). We will retain the practice of rachatz (washing hands with a blessing before the meal) because of its probable link to Jesus' radical act of washing his disciples' feet during the Last Supper.

15 Scripture is filled with references to the righteous nature of the right hand. After

Two ritual objects on the seder table perhaps capture the most attention and imagination: the seder plate and the Cup of Elijah, both of which are ornately decorated.

The Seder Plate

The key symbols of Passover are grouped, sometimes in small dishes, on the seder plate (or platter) placed on the table in front of the leader. The leader will explain the significance of everything on the plate during the seder:

✧ *Beitzah*: roasted hardboiled egg, symbolizes the regular festival Temple.

✧ *Z'ro-a*: roasted lamb shank bone, symbolizes the sacrificial lamb eaten in ancient times.

✧ *Moror*: bitter herbs — usually horseradish, freshly grated or very finely sliced — symbolize the bitter life ancient Hebrews led as slaves in Egypt. Contemporary Jews recognize this as a symbol for enslaved people everywhere.

✧ *Karpas*: greens — usually parsley — symbolize Passover as the Festival of Spring as well as the Festival of Freedom and Deliverance.

✧ *Charoses*: chopped apple and nut mixture, symbolizes mortar used by enslaved Hebrews to build Egyptian cities.

---

passing through the Red Sea, Moses and the Israelites sing, "Your right hand, O Lord, was majestic in power. Your right hand shattered the enemy" (Exodus 15:6). The psalmist sings, "The Lord is at your right hand; he will crush kings on the day of his wrath" (Psalm 110:5). Each of the Synoptic Gospels reports Jesus facing the Sanhedrin after his arrest and declaring that as the Christ and the Son of God, "... the Son of Man will be seated at the right hand of the mighty God..." (Matthew 26:62-64, Mark 14:61-62, Luke 22:67-69). This declaration takes place after the Last Supper at which, being an observant Jew, Jesus would have followed this custom of lounging and leaning to the left.

Place three matzot, either tucked into the three sections of a special matzoh cover or within the folds of a cloth napkin, to the right of the seder plate.

As you set your table, remember to include little individual dishes of salt water and enough extra moror, karpas, and charoses for each person to taste and enjoy during the seder. For larger groups, place additional seder plates where everyone can easily see them.

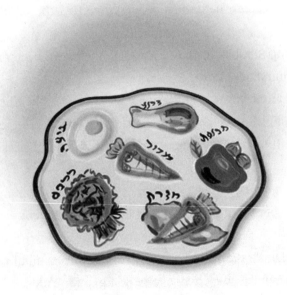

The Cup of Elijah

Reserve the place of honor at the table's center for the Cup of Elijah.[16] This ornate goblet should be accompanied by a small carafe of wine. More about this custom is revealed during the seder. An empty armchair symbolizes a place for Elijah.

See, I will send you the prophet Elijah before that
great and dreadful day of the Lord comes.
MALACHI 4:5

PREPARING THE HEART

Passover falls during Lent, a sacred time of reflection and recollection. During the forty days of Lent, we're called to become more inwardly focused. As Christians, we're invited to renounce whatever distracts us from living the Gospel teachings of love, generosity, and service.

Lent is also a time for reconciliation. Activities of the season (e.g., praying Stations of the Cross; the custom in some parishes of holding a parish-wide penance service) call us to consider where, when, and how we've been out of alignment with our faith. In the stillness of prayer, we prepare our hearts to receive the miracle of death defied and God's promise fulfilled through the resurrection of Christ Jesus.

For Passover, we prepare home and table to remember our ancestors' liberation from Egyptian bondage. We also prepare our hearts to be released from the bondage of ignorance, confusion, and any misunderstanding that keeps us from full reconciliation with the Jewish community. In answer to the customary question, "What are

---

16   In recent years, especially with the admission of women to the Conservative, Reform, and Reconstructionist rabbinate, there has been a movement to include a "Cup of Miriam" to honor the prophet, sister of Moses and Aaron.

After they safely walked through the miraculously parted Red Sea to dry land, Miriam led the women and "with tambourine and dancing ... sang to them: 'Sing to the Lord, for he is highly exalted. The horse and its rider he has hurled into the sea'" (Exodus 15:20-21).

The Cup of Miriam is obviously an inclusive gesture, but as one friend of mine, a woman, ironically observed, "Oy, why a cup? At least put a tambourine on the table."

you giving up for Lent?" consider declaring that you've renounced any beliefs, attitudes, and behaviors that get in the way of interfaith reconciliation.

"Do you think that I have come to abolish the Law or the Prophets;
I have not come to abolish them but to fulfill them. I tell you the truth,
until heaven and earth disappear, not the smallest letter,
nor the least stroke of a pen, will by any means disappear
from the Law until everything is accomplished... ."
MATTHEW 5:17

ORDER OF SERVICE

THE TRADITIONAL SEDER

KIDDUSH
> *The Cup of Sanctification*

URCHATZ
> *Washing Hands without a Blessing*

KARPAS
> *Blessing the Greens*

YACHATZ
> *Dividing the Matzot*

MAGGID
> *Reciting the Passover Story*
> > *The Four Questions*
> > *The Story of Deliverance from Egyptian Bondage*
> > *Dayenu*

THE CATHOLIC PASSOVER SEDER

KIDDUSH

The Cup of Sanctification

KARPAS

Blessing the Greens

MAGGID

Reciting the Passover Story

The Four Questions

The Story of Deliverance from Egyptian Bondage

The Three Symbols of Passover

Hallel (Psalms 113 and 114)*

The Cup of Redemption

RACHATZ

Blessing the Washing of Hands

MOTZI MATZOH

Blessing the Matzoh

MOROR

Blessing the Bitter Herbs

SHULHAN OREKH

Eating the Festival Meal

BOREKH

Grace

The Cup of Blessing*

The Cup of Elijah

HALLEL

    Psalms of Praise*

    The Cup of Acceptance

NIRTZEH

     Closing prayer

      Our Cup of Salvation

*May be omitted when there are time constraints.

IV

A CATHOLIC PASSOVER SEDER

Leader   We begin our Catholic Passover seder by lighting holiday
candles.[17]

*In Judaism, women have the privilege of lighting and blessing holiday
candles. Assign this* mitzvah[18] *to the family matriarch or to a senior
woman in your faith community.*

---

17 We begin our Easter Vigil Mass with the Service of Light, which involves lighting and blessing the Easter candle from the new fire and then reciting or
singing the Easter Proclamation (*Exsultet*) that includes the words, "Accept this
Easter candle. May it always dispel the darkness of this night! May the morning star which never sets find this flame still burning: Christ, that morning star,
who came back from the dead, and shed his peaceful light, your son who lives
and reigns for ever and ever. Amen."

18 In his book, *What Do Jews Believe?* (Shocken, 1995: 204), David Ariel describes
women's unique home-based ritual obligations that emerged after the Second

Woman Blessed are you, O Lord our God, King of the Universe
who has commanded us to light the festival lights.[19]

Blessed are you, O Lord our God, King of the Universe,
who has given us life, sustained us, and brought us to
this celebration.

All Amen.

Leader Tonight, we recite an ancient story of liberation. It's the
story of miracles and redemption that Our Lord Jesus
and his disciples studied the night before his crucifixion.

When we recount how the Israelites escaped Egyptian
bondage, we join all throughout the ages who have been
called to commemorate God's faithfulness and deliverance from bondage. As followers of Jesus, we celebrate
God's enduring and infinite mercy for all.

(Leader points to the seder plate.)

This is a seder plate. On it are the symbols of Passover.

Temple was destroyed in 70 CE. Candle lighting at sundown before the Sabbath
and other holidays begin is among these specific *mitzvot* (commandments).

19 Hebrew blessings always begin with: "*Barukh atah Adonai, eloheinu melekh ha-
olam* (Blessed are You, O Lord our God, King of the Universe.") This is as sacro-
sanct as reciting the Latin words of the *Kyrie* or *Agnus Dei*. As with everything
else in Judaism, there's a reason (born of debate) for the grammatical weird-
ness. Rabbi Hayim Halevy Donin explains all this in *To Pray as a Jew: A Guide to
the Prayer Book and the Synagogue Service* (Basic Books, 1980: 65-67): "We begin
in the second person, addressing God as '*atah*,' Thou, or You, when we relate
to Him as our Father, as the source of mercy and compassion, as the One who
cares for mankind. This sense of nearness to God, in fact, is essential to Jewish prayer.... We become more formal and conclude the blessing in the third
person, 'who sanctified us...' or 'who created the fruit of the earth.' When we
relate to God as a Sovereign Ruler, we assume a more respectful role."

(Leader lifts the three matzot.)

These three matzot represent the bread that sustained our forebears as they fled from Egypt. According to tradition, these three matzot also represent the major social divisions among our biblical ancestors: priests (Kohanim), associate priests (Levites), and laity (Israelites).[20]

(Leader lifts the roasted shank bone.)

This roasted shank bone represents the lamb that was ritually sacrificed and offered at the Temple of Jerusalem during Passover.[21] For us, the lamb symbolizes Jesus Christ, the Lamb of God — unblemished and whole — whose self-sacrifice takes away the sins of the world and triumphs over death.

(Leader lifts the roasted egg.)

The egg is a universal symbol of life. This one represents another festival offering, traditionally presented at the Temple of Jerusalem during Passover. Roasted, it also symbolizes the destruction of the Second Temple of

---

20   You'll find an accounting of the tribes of Israel and the social roles assigned by God through Moses in Numbers 1-6.

21   Key events in Jesus' life are tied to this annual feast at the Temple of Jerusalem. Luke's Gospel (2:41-49) recalls how one year, twelve-year-old Jesus was inadvertently left behind. Mary and Joseph return to Jerusalem and, after frantically searching, find the boy sitting in discourse among the rabbis. "Why were you searching for me?" he asked. "Didn't you know I had to be in my Father's house?"

John's Gospel (2:13-19) tells about the adult Jesus driving cattlemen and moneychangers from the Temple of Jerusalem right before Passover. "Get these out of here! How dare you turn my Father's house into a market!" When his authority to do this is challenged by authorities, Jesus answers, "Destroy this temple, and I will raise it again in three days."

Jerusalem. For those with Easter faith, the egg represents Christ's emergence from the stone tomb into life everlasting.[22]

(Leader lifts a slice of horseradish.)
Moror, a bitter herb, reminds us of the harshness of slavery when eating it brings tears to our eyes.

(Leader points to the charoses.)
Charoses, made with apples and nuts symbolizes mortar mixed and used by our ancestors who, as slave labor, built the cities and pyramids of ancient Egypt.

(Leader lifts a sprig of parsley.)
This is karpas, a reminder of springtime and its bounty.

(Leader points to the carafe of wine.)
We will drink four glasses of wine during the seder.
Each represents, in part, God's promises as revealed in Exodus (6:6-7):[23]
✧ I will bring you out from under the yoke of the Egyptians.

---

22 According to legend, Mary Magdalene's story about Jesus' resurrection was challenged by the Roman emperor Tiberius who said that no one could rise from the dead any more than an egg could turn red. As Mary Magdalene picked an egg up from the table, it turned bright red. Today, Eastern Rite Christians honor this story by coloring Easter eggs bright red. Icons of Mary Magdalene often show her holding an egg.

23 God is a God of promises made and promises kept. In Genesis, God establishes a covenant with Noah to protect every living creature (Genesis 9:8-17) and makes a land covenant with Abram [Abraham] (Genesis 15:12-21). This latter promise along with these four (Exodus 6:6-7), provide the scriptural basis for understanding God's unique relationship with the Jewish people.

> ✧ I will free you from being slaves to them.
>
> ✧ I will redeem you with an outstretched arm and
>   with mighty acts of judgment.
>
> ✧ I will take you as my own people, and will be your God.

Leader   These symbols of Passover remind us of a time of great
suffering. Tonight, we remember that God's promise of
freedom endures, even in the face of oppression and our
human resistance to deliverance and salvation.

KIDDUSH
The First Cup: The Cup of Sanctification

Leader   Please bow your head as we sanctify this Passover
service by reciting the traditional blessing over wine.

*(In a large group, designate someone to pour the first cup of wine for
everyone at each table.)*

Together, we pray:

All   Blessed are you, O Lord our God, King of the Universe
who creates the fruit of the vine. Amen.

But also worthy of contemplation is God's promise to King David as
revealed to Nathan: "'When your days are over and you go to be with your
fathers, I will raise up your offspring to succeed you, one of your own sons,
and I will establish his kingdom. He is the one who will build a house for me,
and I will establish his throne forever. I will be his father, and he will be my
son. I will never take my love away from him, as I took it away from your pred-
ecessor. I will set him over my house and my kingdom forever; his throne will
be established forever.'" (1 Chronicles 17:11-14) Christian theologians view this
Davidic Covenant as heralding Christ Jesus.

(Participants drink the first cup of wine.)
Leader   Please be seated.

KARPAS
Blessing the Greens

(Leader distributes a sprig of parsley to participants.)
Leader   We thank God for renewing the earth each spring. Before
eating the karpas, we pray:

All   Blessed are you, O Lord our God, King of the Universe,
who creates the fruit of the earth. Amen.

(Participants eat the karpas.)

MAGGID
Reciting the Passover Story

(Leader uncovers one of the three matzot and lifts it up.)
Leader   Behold, this is the bread of affliction that our ancestors
ate after they fled from Egypt.

All   Let all who are hungry, come and eat this bread.
May we share our earthly and spiritual sustenance with
all people. Let all who are oppressed, be liberated from
bondage. May we all know true freedom and peace.

(Leader lowers and covers the matzot. The second cup of wine is poured.)

Jesus said to them, "I tell you the truth, it is not Moses who has given you the bread from heaven, but it is my Father who gives you the true bread from heaven. For the bread of God is he who comes down from heaven and gives life to the world." "Sir," they said, "from now on give us this bread." Then Jesus declared, "I am the bread of life. He who comes to me will never go hungry..."

JOHN 6:32–35

The Four Questions

Traditionally, the youngest participant at the seder asks the Four Questions. You can easily follow this custom in a private home. In a group setting, designate someone in advance to ask these questions.

Child   I have four questions to ask:

Why is this night different from all other nights?

✧ On all other nights, we may eat either regular bread or unleavened bread. Why, on this night, do we eat only unleavened bread?

✧ On all other nights, we may eat all kinds of herbs. Why, on this night, do we eat only bitter herbs?

✧ On all other nights, we do not dip herbs at all. Why, on this night, do we dip the karpas in salt water?

✧ On all other nights, we may eat either sitting or reclining. Why, on this night, do we recline?

Leader   For thousands of years, these questions have been asked at seders, traditionally by the youngest. During the Last

Supper, it probably was John, the youngest disciple of Jesus. The answers reveal God's special relationship with the Jewish people.

Tonight, as followers of Christ Jesus, we retell these stories of slavery and liberation, oppression, and redemption to remind us of God's eternal grace and mercy.

In large communities, readers are appointed in advance. At family seders, all participants read from their haggadot and simply pass the process of reading out loud around the table.

Reader   Tonight, we eat only unleavened bread because our ancestors had to flee Egypt so quickly, they could not wait for their dough to rise.

Tonight, we eat only bitter herbs to remember the bitterness of the slavery and oppression our ancestors endured.

Tonight, we dip greens in salt water, a symbol of tears our forebears cried from pain, grief, and despair.

Tonight, we combine bitter herbs with sweet charoses to remind us that life is both bitter and sweet.

Tonight, we recline because we are no longer slaves, but free to relax and enjoy our holiday meal.

Leader   This passage from Deuteronomy (6:21–22) explains why these four questions must be answered tonight:

Reader   "In the future, when anyone asks, 'What is the meaning of the stipulations, decrees, and laws the Lord our God has commanded you?' you are to reply: 'We were slaves of Pharaoh in Egypt, but the Lord brought us out of Egypt with a mighty hand. Before our eyes the Lord sent miraculous signs and wonders — great and terrible — upon Egypt and Pharaoh and his whole household." [24]

The Story of Deliverance from Egyptian Bondage

Leader   We find the story of deliverance from Egyptian bondage in Exodus (1–15) and again in Deuteronomy (26:5–9). And yet, this story really begins in Genesis where we read about being in bondage to images and superstitions. In Genesis, God calls Abram[25] into relationship and makes an eternal covenant with him and all his descendants.

God said: "Know for certain that your descendants will be strangers in a country not their own, and they will be enslaved and mistreated for four hundred years. But I will punish the nation they serve as slaves, and afterward they will come out with great possessions" (Genesis 15:13–14).

---

24   *Torah* (teaching) primarily refers to the Pentateuch, the Five Books of Moses (Genesis, Exodus, Leviticus, Numbers, and Deuteronomy), the core of Hebrew Scriptures or *Tanahkh*. In addition to Torah, the Tanakh includes Nevi'im (The Prophets) and Ketuvim (The Writings). Jews refer to the Tanakh as either "The Holy Scriptures" or "The Bible," but never "The Old Testament." The distinction between "Hebrew Scriptures" and "Christian Scriptures" was proposed by Pope John Paul II to eliminate the implication that the Old Testament was rendered somehow obsolete by the birth, death, and resurrection of Jesus Christ. If you hold that the entirety of scripture is a compilation that expresses ever-developing belief, then Christian reference to "the Bible" makes sense.

Regarding this story of deliverance, even if you have never read Exodus, you'd still find it in the Christian Scriptures. Stephen, a Greek-speaking Jew who became the Church's first martyr recounted this history to the Sanhedrin (Acts 7:17-36) to answer charges of blasphemy against Moses and God.

Reader   In Exodus, we learn how our ancestors became a great, flourishing nation within Egypt. We read about a new king coming into power. Fearing the Israelites, this pharaoh tried to suppress them, first through hard labor and then by murdering their newborn sons. Midwives defied these orders and more Israelites were safely born.

One mother swaddled her baby boy, placed him in a papyrus basket, and floated him among the reeds of the Nile. Her son was rescued by Pharaoh's daughter; she named him Moses, meaning "to draw out."

As years passed, Moses would see the oppression of his own people. He'd kill an Egyptian for abusing a Hebrew slave and then flee to live as a shepherd in Midian. One day, God revealed himself to Moses from within a bush that burned but was not destroyed by its flames.

God said to Moses: "And now the cry of the Israelites has reached me, and I have seen the way the Egyptians are oppressing them. So now, go. I am sending you to Pharaoh to bring my people, the Israelites, out of Egypt" (Exodus 3:9–10).

As written in Deuteronomy (26:8):

"So the Lord brought us out of Egypt with a mighty hand and an outstretched arm, with great terror and with miraculous signs and wonders." [26]

---

25   Throughout scripture, names change at times of great transformation in identity and relationship to God and God's people. In Genesis, Abram (exalted father) becomes Abraham (father of many) when God promises the land of Canaan to him and all his descendants (Genesis 17:5-8). In Acts, Saul of Tarsus encounters a vision of Jesus on the road to Damascus and is transformed from being a feared persecutor of Christian Jews to Paul, apostle for Christ (Acts 9:1-28).

Leader   Not until the Angel of Death slaughtered all Egyptian firstborn sons, did Pharaoh summon Moses and his brother Aaron, saying "Up! Leave my people, you and the Israelites! Go, worship the Lord as you have requested. ..." (Exodus 12:31).[27]

In Exodus (12:40–41) we read: "The length of time the Israelites lived in Egypt was 430 years. At the end of the 430 years, to the very day, all the ranks of the Lord departed from the land of Egypt."

All   "Because the Lord kept vigil that night to bring them out of Egypt, on this night all the Israelites are to keep vigil to honor the Lord for the generations to come" (Exodus 12:42).

The Three Symbols of Passover

Leader   During the first century, Rabbi Gamaliel, revered teacher of Saul of Tarsus who would become the Apostle Paul, declared: "Those who do not study the three symbols of

---

26   Imagine the horror of Pharaoh, the self-proclaimed embodiment of God, who could do nothing to save his people as blood flowed in the rivers, hail fell from the sky, locusts devoured the crops, bodies erupted in boils, and Egyptian first-born males mysteriously and swiftly died.

27   The traditional seder narrative ends at this point. During Easter Vigil, the Exodus story continues. Of the seven Bible readings assigned to Easter Vigil, Exodus 14:15-15:1 may never be omitted. This reading begins with events surrounding God's miraculous rescue of the Israelites at the banks of the Red Sea, and ends with Miriam's victory song. Reinforcing our belief that crossing the Red Sea prefigured salvation by baptism, one suggested prayer after this reading includes the affirmation: "You once saved a single nation from slavery, and now you offer that salvation to all through baptism" (see also: CCC 1094-1095).

Passover — Z'ro-a, matzoh, and moror — have not fulfilled their duty." Tonight, we examine these symbols more closely.

(Leader lifts or points to the roasted shank bone, z'roa, on the seder plate.)

This roasted bone represents the Paschal lamb, the ancient Passover sacrifice. Torah (Exodus 12:5–14) tells how on the night before escaping Egypt, our forebears were told to slaughter a perfect lamb, mark the door frames of their homes with its blood,[28] and then roast it with bitter herbs. This Passover offering would have to be eaten quickly.

Reader   God said: "For on that night I will go throughout Egypt, striking down every firstborn — both human and animal.

---

28   This biblical injunction has been distorted into the blood libel or false charge that Jews would use the blood of a slaughtered Christian boy to prepare matzoh. Perhaps the earliest recorded blood libel was spread during the twelfth century. In 1171, thirty Jews were executed by burning for this fabricated crime in the French city of Blois.

Blood libels were especially rampant throughout Europe during the Middle Ages. *The Universal Jewish Encyclopedia* lists the locations of 140 blood libel trials. Blood libels have been used to persecute Jews, especially during Holy Week, as recently as the twentieth century. The blood libel spread to the Middle East during the eighteenth century and has emerged there again in the wake of Israeli–Palestinian conflict during our own times, the twenty-first century.

On occasion, certain popes (most notably Pope Gregory X during the thirteenth century and Pope Benedict XIV during the eighteenth) issued statements against blood libels, but the Catholic Church didn't officially recant them until after the Second Vatican Council. Nonetheless, the Fried-Bread Procession in Tierno, Italy, and the Domenichino Festival in Fobruomo, Spain, both anchored in anti-Semitic legend, are still celebrated.

I will bring judgment on all the gods of Egypt. I am the Lord" (Exodus 12:12).

God said: "The blood on the houses where you live will be a sign for you: when I see the blood I will *pass over* you, so that no plague will destroy you when I strike Egypt" (Exodus 12:13).[29]

Leader As Christians, we now recall this message delivered by John the Baptist (John 1:29–31):

"Behold, the Lamb of God, who takes away the sin of the world! This is the one I meant when I said, 'A man who comes after me has surpassed me.' I myself did not know him, but the reason I came baptizing with water was that he might be revealed to Israel."

Leader

(Lifts a piece of matzoh from the seder plate.)

This matzoh represents the unleavened bread our forebears ate. In Exodus (12:39) we read: "And they baked cakes of unleavened bread of the dough that they had taken out of Egypt. The dough was without yeast because they had been driven out of Egypt and did not have time to prepare food for themselves."

---

29 The children of Israel are spared certain death by the blood of a male lamb without blemish. As Christians, we believe that all sins have been forgiven; we are liberated from death, and brought into eternal life by the blood of Jesus Christ, Lamb of God. Listen to Peter's assurances to early Christians being persecuted in Asia Minor: "It was not with perishable things such as silver and gold that you were redeemed from an empty way of life, but with the precious blood of Christ, a lamb without blemish or defect. ...Through him you believe in God, who raised him from the dead and glorified him, and so your faith and hope are in God" (1 Peter 1:18-19, 21).

As Christians, we now recall the instructions the Apostle Paul delivered to squabbling members of the early church in Corinth (1 Corinthians 5:6–8):

Reader   "Don't you know that a little yeast works through the whole batch of dough? Get rid of the old yeast that you may be a new batch without yeast — as you really are. For Christ, our Passover lamb has been sacrificed. Therefore let us keep the festival, not with the old yeast, the yeast of malice and wickedness, but with bread made without yeast, the bread of sincerity and truth."

Leader

(Lifts some bitter herbs from the seder plate.)

These bitter herbs reminds us of our enslaved forebears. Exodus (1:14) tells how the Egyptians hated the Israelites: "They made their lives bitter with hard labor in brick and mortar and with all kinds of work in the fields; in all their hard labor the Egyptians used them ruthlessly."

Consider these verses from Paul's letter to the early church in Rome (Romans 8:38–39):[30]

Reader   "Neither death nor life, neither angels nor demons, neither the present nor the future, nor any powers, neither height nor depth, nor anything else in all creation, will be able to separate us from the love of God that is in Christ Jesus our Lord."

---

30 Note the prophecy in Revelation (21:4-5) about the New Jerusalem who is Christ Jesus: "He will wipe every tear from their eyes. There will be no more death or mourning or crying or pain, for the old order of things has passed away. He who was seated on the throne said, 'I am making everything new!'"

HALLEL

Psalms of thanks and praise are chanted before and after the meal. Only Psalms 113 and 114 [31] *are recited or chanted before the meal.*

PSALM 113

All   Let the name of the Lord be praised, now and forever.

Reader   Praise the Lord!

O servants of the Lord, sing praise;

praise the name of the Lord.

Let the name of the Lord be praised,

now and forever.

From east to west

the name of the Lord is to be praised.

All   Let the name of the Lord be praised, now and forever.

Reader   The Lord is exalted above all nations,

God's glory extends beyond the heavens.

Who is like the Lord our God,

who, enthroned on high,

sees what is below in heaven and on earth?

All   Let the name of the Lord be praised,

now and forever.

---

31   The word *hallelu* (praise) *jah* (the Lord). To reinforce the penitential aspects of Lent, we do not sing the Alleluia before the Gospel reading nor in any song, hymn, or anthem. This joyful acclamation returns during the Easter Vigil when we celebrate the Risen Lord.

Reader   God raises the poor from the dust,
          lifts the needy from despair;
          to seat them with the powerful among God's people.
          God transforms the childless woman to a happy mother.

All   Let the name of the Lord be praised,
          now and forever.

PSALM 114

All   Tremble, O earth, at the presence of the Lord.

Reader   When Israel came out of Egypt,
          the house of Jacob from an alien people,
          Judah became God's sanctuary,
          Israel, God's dominion.

All   Tremble, O earth, at the presence of the Lord.

Reader   The sea looked and fled,
          Jordan flowed backward,
          mountains skipped like rams,
          hills like lambs.

All   Tremble, O earth, at the presence of the Lord.

Reader   Why was it, O sea, that you fled?
          O Jordan, that you retreated?
          you mountains, that you skipped like rams,
          you hills, like lambs?

All   Tremble, O earth, at the presence of the Lord.

Reader   Tremble, O earth, at the presence of the Lord,
at the presence of Jacob's God
who turned rocks into pools of water,
flint rock into flowing fountains.

The Second Cup: The Cup of Redemption

(*Participants raise wine cups with their right hands.*)

All   Blessed are you, O Lord our God, King of the Universe,
who has redeemed us and our ancestors from Egypt,
and brought us to this night.

O Lord, Our God, may you bring us to more holy days
and celebrations in peace. May we rejoice in your right-
eousness. May all your people come together in peace to
know and do your will.

Leader   Again, we recite the traditional blessing over the wine:

All   Blessed are you, O Lord our God, King of the Universe,
who creates the fruit of the vine. Amen.

(*Participants drink the second cup of wine.*)

RACHATZ
Blessing the Washing of Hands

Leader   At this point in the traditional seder, a hand-washing ritual takes place. As Christians, we now remember when, during the Last Supper, Jesus, already knowing who will betray him, rose from the table, and bathed his disciples' feet.

Reader   A reading from the Gospel according to John (13:2–17): "When Jesus had finished washing their feet, he put on his clothes and returned to his place. 'Do you understand what I have done for you?' he asked them. 'You call me "Teacher" and "Lord," and rightly so, for that is what I am. Now that I, your Lord and Teacher, have washed your feet, you also should wash one another's feet. I have set you an example of what you should do as I have done for you. I tell you the truth, no servant is greater than his master, nor is a messenger greater than the one who sent him: Now that you know these things, you will be blessed if you do them.'"

MOTZI MATZOH
Blessing the Matzoh

(Leader breaks the upper and middle matzot into small pieces and distributes them to the participants.)

Leader   Together, we pray:

All   Blessed are you, O Lord our God, King of the Universe, who brings forth bread from the earth. Blessed are you, O Lord our God, King of the Universe, who sanctifies our life by your commandments, and commands us to eat unleavened bread. Amen.

(Participants eat the matzoh.)

MOROR
Blessing the Bitter Herbs

(Everyone takes a little of the bitter herbs and charoses.)

Leader   As we eat the moror and charoses, we remember how the bitterness of slavery is sweetened by redemption. We pray:

All   Blessed are you, Our God, Rule of the Universe, who sanctifies our lives by your commandments, and commands us to eat the bitter herbs. Amen.

(Participants eat the bitter herbs and charoses. How? By dipping parsley into the charoses.)

SHULHAN OREKH
Remove the Seder Plate and Serve the Festival Meal!

When the hour came, Jesus and his apostles reclined at the table. And he said to them, "I have eagerly desired to eat this passover with you before I suffer. For I tell you, I will not eat it again until it finds fulfillment in the kingdom of God."

After taking the cup, he gave thanks and said, "Take this and divide it among you. For I tell you, I will not drink again of the fruit of the vine until the kingdom of God comes."

And he took bread, gave thanks and broke it, and gave it to them, saying, "This is my body given for you; do this in remembrance of me."

LUKE 22:15–19

The Seder Continues after Completing the Meal

BOREKH
Grace

(Refill wine cups a third time.)

Leader   We offer thanks to God for the food we have eaten.
Tonight our response will be: Blessed are you, Our God.
We praise you, God, for the food and fellowship we
have enjoyed.

All   Blessed are you, Our God.

Leader   We thank you, God, for the privilege of recalling
Passover.

All   Blessed are you, Our God.

Leader   God, your kindness, mercy, and compassion are endless.
You are forever faithful and your goodness fills all time
and space.

All   Blessed are you, Our God.

The Third Cup: The Cup of Blessing

(Participants raise wine cups with their right hands.)

Leader   Remembering God's third promise: "I will redeem you with an outstretched hand," we recite the traditional blessing over the wine:

All   Blessed are you, O Lord our God, King of the Universe, who creates the fruit of the vine. Amen.

(Participants drink the third cup of wine.)

The Cup of Elijah

(Leader points to the Cup of Elijah.)

Leader   The Cup of Elijah has a special place on the Passover table, just as the prophet Elijah holds a special place at the heart of mystery.

At traditional seder celebrations, a child opens the front door to symbolically welcome the prophet Elijah, who heralds the coming Messiah.

Reader   A reading from the Gospel according to Matthew (17:1–8):

"After six days Jesus took with him Peter, James, and John the brother of James, and led them up a high mountain by themselves. There he was transfigured before them. His face shone like the sun, and his clothes became as white as the light. Just then there appeared before them Moses and Elijah, talking with Jesus. Peter said to Jesus, 'Lord, it is good for us to be here. If you wish, I will put up three shelters — one for you, one for Moses, and one for Elijah.'

"While he was still speaking, a bright cloud enveloped them, and a voice from the cloud said, 'This is my Son,

whom I love; with him I am well pleased. Listen to him!'
"When the disciples heard this, they fell face down to
the ground, terrified. But Jesus came and touched them.
'Get up,' he said. 'Do not be afraid.' When they looked
up, they saw no one except Jesus."

Leader   Tonight, we open the door for Elijah to symbolize our
joyful hope that Christ will come again in glory.[32] As
Jesus tells us in the Gospel according to Matthew
(24:42): "Keep watch, because you do not know on what
day your Lord will come."

(The child opens the door briefly.)

HALLEL
Psalms of Praise

PSALM 116 [33]
(Also chanted on Monday and Thursday of Holy Week.)

All   For you, O Lord, have delivered my soul.

---

32 From the Profession of Faith: "We believe in one God, the Father, the Almighty,
maker of heaven and earth, of all that is seen and unseen. We believe in one
Lord, Jesus Christ, the only Son of God, eternally begotten of the Father, God
from God, Light from Light, true God from true God, begotten, not made, one
in Being with the Father. Through him all things were made. For us and for our
salvation he came down from heaven, by the power of the Holy Spirit he was
born of the Virgin Mary, and became man. For our sake he was crucified under
Pontius Pilate; he suffered, died, and was buried. He descended to the dead.
On the third day he rose again in fulfillment of the scriptures; he ascended into
heaven and is seated at the right hand of the Father. He will come again in
glory to judge the living and the dead, and his kingdom will have no end..."

Reader   I love you Lord, for you hear my voice,
              my cry for mercy.
              You turn your ear to me, whenever I call.
              The cords of death entangled me;
              the anguish of the grave engulfed me.
              I was overcome by trouble and sorrow,
              then I called on you:
              "O Lord, save me!"

All   For you, O Lord, have delivered my soul.

Reader   The Lord is gracious and righteous;
              our God is compassionate.
              The Lord protects the simple;
              when I was in great need, God saved me.

All   For you, O Lord, have delivered my soul.

Reader   Be at rest, once more, O my soul,
              for the Lord is good.
              You, O Lord, have delivered me from death,
              my eyes from tears,
              my feet from stumbling.
              I shall walk before the Lord
              in the lands of the living.

---

33 Traditionally, Psalms 115, 116, 117, 118, and 136 are recited during the second
    half of the seder. In practice, only the extremely devout — and awake after all
    the food and wine — ever get around to reciting them. Indeed, Jesus would
    have led the disciples in singing Psalm 136 in its entirety. It's probably this
    song that gospel writers Matthew (26:30) and Mark (14:26) allude to when
    they report this event: "When they had sung a hymn, they went out to the
    Mount of Olives."

I believe in the Lord;
yet out of great suffering I said,
"No man can be trusted."

All   For you, O Lord, have delivered my soul.

Reader   How can I repay you, Lord
for all your goodness to me?
I will lift up the cup of salvation
and call upon your name.
I will fulfill my vows to you, Lord
in the presence of all your people.

The death of saints is precious in your sight.
O Lord,
I am your servant;
I am your servant, the son of your maidservant;
You have freed me from my chains.

All   For you, O Lord, have delivered my soul.

Reader   I will sacrifice a thanks offering to you
and call upon your name.
I will fulfill my vows to you
in the presence of your people,
in the courts of the house of the Lord,
in the midst of Jerusalem.
Hallelujah.

All   For you, O Lord, have delivered my soul.

PSALM 118

(Chanted or recited during Easter Vigil and Easter Sunday.)

All   You are my God and I will give you thanks.

Reader   Give thanks to the Lord, for God is good,
               God's love endures forever.
               Let Israel declare:
               "God's love endures forever."
               Let the house of Aaron say:
               "God's love endures forever."
               Let those who fear the Lord say:
               "God's love endures forever."

All   You are my God and I will give you thanks.

Reader   In anguish I cried out to the Lord,
               who answered by setting me free.
               The Lord is with me,
               I am fearless;
               what can anyone do to me?
               With the Lord on my side as my helper,
               I will see my enemies defeated.
               It is better to take refuge in the Lord
               than to trust in mortals;
               it is better to take refuge in the Lord
               than to trust in the great.

All   You are my God and I will give you thanks.

Reader All the nations surrounded me,
    but in the name of the Lord I will surely cut them down.
    They surrounded me on every side,
    but in the name of the Lord I will surely cut them down.
    They swarmed around me like bees;
    but will die as quickly as burning thorns;
    in the name of the Lord I will surely cut them down.

All You are my God and I will give you thanks.

Reader I was pushed hard and nearly fell,
    but the Lord helped me.
    The Lord is my strength and might;
    God has become my salvation.
    Shouts of joy and victory resound
    in the tents of the righteous:
    "The Lord's right hand has done mighty things!
    The Lord's right hand is lifted high;
    the Lord's right hand has done mighty things!"

All You are my God and I will give you thanks.

Reader I will not die but live
    and proclaim what the Lord has done.
    The Lord has punished me severely,
    but did not give me over to death.
    Open for me the gates of righteousness
    that I may enter and give thanks to the Lord.
    This is the gateway to the Lord —
    through which the righteous may enter.

I will praise you, for you have answered me,
and have become my salvation.

All   You are my God and I will give you thanks.

Reader   The stone that the builders rejected
has become the cornerstone.
This is the Lord's doing;
and it is marvelous in our sight.
This is the day the Lord has made —
let us rejoice and be glad in it.

All   You are my God and I will give you thanks.

Reader   O Lord, save us;
O Lord, let us prosper.
Blessed are those come in the name of the Lord.
From the house of the Lord we bless you.
The Lord is God,
giving us light;
binding the festal offering to the altar with cords.

You are my God and I will praise you;
You are my God and I will exalt you.
Praise the Lord for he is good,
and God's love endures forever.

All   You are my God and I will give you thanks.

The Fourth Cup: The Cup of Acceptance

(Participants raise wine cups with their right hands.)

Leader   Again, we recite the traditional blessing over the wine. This time, we will not drink the entire cup. As followers of Jesus, our commemoration of Passover and Last Supper must end — and continue — in a different way:

All   Blessed are you, O Lord our God, King of the Universe, who creates the fruit of the vine. Amen.

(Participants drink half the wine in their wine cups.)

NIRTZEH
Closing Prayer

Leader   Jewish members of God's family end the seder with a prayer of thanksgiving and hope for universal peace and understanding. This is also a prayer for their symbolic return to Jerusalem. Tonight, we join their prayers with our own for reconciliation and healing among all God's people.

Jesus Christ is, for us, the New Jerusalem.[34] As follow-

---

34   Revelation 21:1-3: "Then I saw a new heaven and a new earth, for the first heaven and earth had passed away, and there was no longer any sea. I saw the Holy City, the New Jerusalem, coming down out of heaven from God. ...And I heard a loud voice from the throne saying, 'Now the dwelling of God is with men, and he will live with them, they will be his people, and God himself will be with them and be their God...'"

ers of Jesus, we will complete our celebration our cup of salvation and contemplate these words from the Gospels:

"After supper had ended, Jesus took the cup, gave thanks and offered it to his disciples, saying, 'This cup is the new covenant in my blood, which is poured out for many for the forgiveness of sins. I tell you the truth; I will not drink of this fruit of the vine from now until the day when I drink it anew with you in my Father's Kingdom.'"

Together, we proclaim the mystery of our faith as we finish this cup of wine.

All   Christ has died.
Christ is risen.
Christ will come again.
Blessed are you, O Lord our God, King of the Universe, who creates the fruit of the vine. Amen.

(Participants finish drinking the wine in their wine cups.)

Leader   Our Catholic Passover seder is ended. Go with humility to observe the solemnities of Holy Week. Go with the joy of knowing that death has been defeated. Go in peace to love and serve God and one another.

All   Thanks be to God.[35]

---

35   This familiar formula of dismissal reminds us how to go forth from Church into daily life. Synagogue services end with this benediction:
"The Lord bless you and keep you;
The Lord make his face to shine upon you and be gracious unto you;
The Lord turn his face toward you and grant you peace."
NUMBERS 6:24-26

APPENDIX A

A PASSOVER CHECKLIST FOR FAITH COMMUNITIES

Planning a seder is a big deal. It's a big deal for an individual family. It's an even bigger big deal when planning for a community. Even if your parish excels at producing pancake breakfasts and spaghetti dinners, you'll need to factor in extra time to handle the inevitable glitches that come with planning something new, different, big, and sacred — with food.

This endeavor most likely will involve coordinating many volunteers, at least some of whom work full-time and have other responsibilities. Adding kids to the volunteer mix presents yet another set of scheduling and managing challenges, as does the number and skills of everyone on your seder preparation committee. You'll need to set up a project team early on. Make sure someone takes on the role of secretary to keep communications flowing. Since this event requires finances, someone will need to be the treasurer. And you'll need back-ups — plans and people — for everything every step of the way. Now would be an excellent time to mention that planning a community seder will provide abundant opportunities for you to see Christ in everyone. (Now also would be an excellent time for me to recommend one of my earlier books, *Deliberate Acts of Kindness: Service as a Spiritual Practice*, Doubleday, especially Chapter 5, "The Shadow Side of Service.")

Up to a year in advance

✧ Decide whether attendees may bring guests from outside the parish, and then do your best to estimate attendance.

✧ Plan a budget and figure out the per-person fee. Decide how to subsidize the cost for attendees who might not be able to afford the fee. If the cost of this event is being covered by the parish, decide if you'll also request a "free will offering" and how much you'll gently suggest it might be.

✧ Schedule the time and reserve a seder location. Even if you use a caterer, you'll need to choose a room that's near a kitchen.

Up to six months in advance

✧ Create publicity materials to include: church bulletin notices, a special flyer/postcard mailing(s), bulletin board materials, and content for your parish website. These materials should highlight the significance of celebrating Passover during Lent. Announce seder date, time, location, and fee.

✧ Enroll volunteers to purchase ingredients and to prepare seder plate items, charoses, desserts, coffee, and tea.

✧ Hire a caterer who has experience preparing Passover meals to provide the soup and matzoh balls, gefilte fish (if you want to go the Ashkenazic route, see Appendix B), the main course, vegetables, and salad. Either plan your menu and then call the caterer, or find a caterer and ask for suggestions. *Note:* Depending on the date of your seder, you may need to accommodate Lenten dietary observances — or, for the sake of interfaith reconciliation, arrange for a dispensation to eat something you may have renounced during Lent!

✧ Enroll volunteers for set up and clean up. Even though your caterer will clean up the kitchen, you'll probably have leftovers to wrap, tables and chairs to put away, tablecloths to get laundered, etc.

✧ Provide volunteer sign-up information in church bulletin or however your parish customarily recruits volunteers.

Two months in advance

✧ Select the primary leader. You might want to choose an experienced Lector or anyone comfortable conveying the meaning of written text while reading out loud. Your leader should be able to command the rapt attention of attendees *and* inspire participation.

✧ Assign key reading and ceremonial roles.

✧ Distribute recipes for whatever foods are being prepared by parish volunteers.

✧ If you opt to use psalmody, select a song leader.

✧ Include registration forms in your church's weekly bulletin every week for the next two months.

One month in advance

✧ Review registration figures and start procuring:

♦ Matzot

♦ Wine

♦ Grape juice

♦ Copies of *Come to the Table* for each participant (please!)

+ Tall candlesticks (2)
+ Candles (2 tall white tapers)
+ Water pitchers
+ Wine carafes
+ Water bowls and cloth towels
+ Ceremonial Cup for Elijah (an ornate silver or crystal goblet)
+ Long tables (use rounds only if you have to)
+ Chairs
+ White tablecloths
+ Table napkins
+ Small cushions
+ Place settings: go ahead and resort to nice quality disposable plates, small bowls for charoses, water goblets, small wine glasses, and flatware, especially if your parish does not have an institutional kitchen and an automatic dishwasher to go with it. Save the china, crystal, and silver for the ceremonial objects.
+ Small (2 oz.) pudding/soufflé cups for salt water
+ Seder plates: you can buy a traditional seder plate just about anywhere these days. They sometimes show up at home décor outlets (of all places). Your local synagogue may have a Judaica shop, and there's always on-line shopping. Plan to have several of these at strategic places on the table(s) so that everyone can see them.
+ Matzoh cover: you may use a white linen napkin.

Three weeks in advance

◇ Close registration so you can plan for food, table settings, chairs, and the like. And after you've established those numbers, increase everything by 5% to account for latecomers.

One week in advance

✧ Issue one last call for registration, then close it! Your caterer will need a head count two days in advance.

✧ Order flowers.

Two days before

✧ If feasible, gather together to cook in the church kitchen to enhance the festival experience. You might also create smaller work groups who could gather in home kitchens for seder preparations.

✧ Prepare in advance:

   ✦ Hard-boiled eggs (to be shelled before serving)

   ✦ Soup (if not provided by caterer)

   ✦ Desserts

   ✦ Charoses

The day

✧ Prepare:

   ✦ Salted water

   ✦ Roasted shank bone

   ✦ Roasted egg

   ✦ Grated/sliced horseradish

   ✦ Salads/side dishes not provided by caterer

✧ Create seder plate(s)

✧ Set tables in a T- or U-shape to maximize the ability for participants to see, hear, and respond to the leader and to each other.

Appendix B

Passover Menus

WHAT will be featured on your menu? Contemplate WWJE (What would Jesus eat?) and WWMC (What would Mary(s) cook?), then take it from there. Generally, the origin of the hosting family will influence whatever shows up on the Passover menu, including ingredients used in at least one ceremonial food (charoses). The Jews from Eastern Europe are called *Ashkenazim*; *Sephardim* are from the Middle East, Spain, or Italy.

And even within those categories, the menu will differ according to whether the family's Ashkenazic heritage is Russian, Romanian, Polish, Hungarian, or yet another country that may no longer exist. And if they're Sephardic? Well, that could include the food preferences of Spanish, Italian, Greek, and African Jews as well as those from what we think of as Middle Eastern countries. While the Ashkenazic menu is more familiar to North American families, the Sephardic menu is more accurate for Jesus of Nazareth.

In practical terms this means the charoses will probably consist of chopped pecans and dried fruits such as dates, apricots, and figs, all of which are mixed with honey, instead of the Ashkenazic version that is simply chopped apples, walnuts, cinnamon, mixed with red wine. Chicken soup with matzoh balls would not be served. Veal would edge out roasted turkey; gefilte fish would not make an appearance at all. Rice would replace potatoes and it's more likely that eggplant and artichokes, rather than asparagus or glazed carrots would be the featured vegetables. A Passover tsimmes of carrots, sweet potatoes, onions, dried prunes, matzoh meal, and flanken is purely an Ashkenazic concoction. Dessert? Almond macaroons!

Where's the lamb? Isn't lamb — real and symbolic — what this holiday is all about? Yes, but ...

Throughout the Middle East, roasted lamb is traditional for all springtime feasts and indeed Exodus 12:8 specifies that a male lamb be sacrificed, roasted, and eaten to celebrate Passover. But in the 1979 edition of her classic cookbook, *The Jewish Holiday Kitchen*, Joan Nathan explains how some Jews refrain from eating any roasted meat during Passover because "of the bitter memory that the Temple sacrifices are no longer possible." Nevertheless, Middle Eastern Jews will eat lamb as long as it's not roasted. "For other Jews," she writes, "exactly the reverse is true: roasted lamb or other roasted food is served to commemorate the ancient sacrifices."

If you're doing the cooking, the cookbooks I've listed below should help. If you're using a caterer, give yourself a huge break and go with one who has handled a seder meal before. Otherwise, you'll be buying cookbooks for your catering company:

Amster, Linda. *The New York Times Jewish Cookbook: More than 825 Traditional & Contemporary Recipes from Around the World.* St. Martin's Press, 2002.

Amster, Linda. *The New York Times Passover Cookbook: More Than 200 Holiday Recipes from Top Chefs and Writers.* Morrow Cookbooks, 1999.

Da Costa, Beatriz and Joyce Eserky Goldstein. *Sephardic Flavors: Jewish Cooking of the Mediterranean.* Chronicle Books, 2000.

Nathan, Joan. *The Jewish Holiday Kitchen: 250 Recipes from Around the World to Make Your Celebrations Special.* Shocken Books, 1998.

Twena, Pamela Grau. *The Sephardic Table: The Vibrant Cooking of the Mediterranean Jews.* Houghton Mifflin, 1998.

ACKNOWLEDGMENTS

My list of acknowledgments tends to run long in books that have taken less than a year to write. This one took six, so observers and advisors have dropped in and out over the years. Still, there has been a steady core who have supported me throughout: Katherine Boyle of Veritas agency and Liz Walter, the editor on *Deliberate Acts of Kindness* and *The Catholic Home* top this list, as does Father James Tunstead Burtchaell. His pointed and frequently hilarious challenges started in the parking lot of Stuart Academy of the Sacred Heart in Princeton, NJ, and continued by phone and email over the years.

I've been guided by those whose knowledge of ritual and the intricacies of Jewish-Catholic relations have enhanced my own: Andy Brereton, Suzin Green and Alan Goldsmith; Deborah and Sol Metzger. Passover seders with the Rickard family were times of significant formation, especially as I entered into full communion with the Roman Catholic Church. Catechetical colleagues at my home parish, the Catholic Community of St. Charles Borromeo in Skillman, NJ, read early drafts: Marianne Caliguire and Ana Sauthoff. During times of identity breakdown I was guided to greater spiritual wholeness by: Monsignor Martin O'Brien and Bruce Reim. And when it looked like this book would never make it into print, I was blessed with creative support from Paul Schindel and the design sensibility of John Burrows.

Over the past few years, I've had the privilege of speaking at churches where I've met parishioners whose interest in all things Catholic is matched by their abiding interest in their Jewish heritage. I thank God for their inspiration; for breathing life into this project whenever I was gasping for air.

NOTES

NOTES